Minibeast Pets
Spiders

by Theresa Greenaway

Photographs by Chris Fairclough

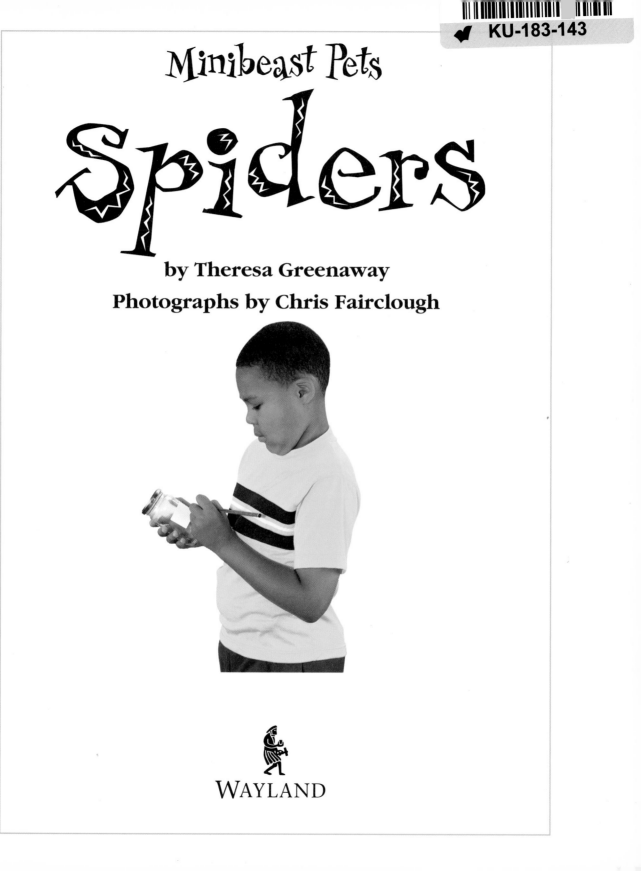

WAYLAND

Minibeast Pets

Caterpillars   Spiders
Slugs and Snails   Worms

Cover photograph: A wasp spider.

All Wayland books encourage
children to read and help them improve their literacy.

✓ The contents page, page numbers, headings, diagrams and index help locate specific pieces of information.

✓ The glossary reinforces alphabetic knowledge and extends vocabulary.

✓ On page 30 you can find out about other books and videos dealing with the same subject.

© Copyright 1999 (text) Wayland Publishers Limited
61 Western Road, Hove, East Sussex BN3 1JD

Planned and produced by Discovery Books Limited
Project Editors: Gianna Williams, Kathy DeVico
Project Manager: Joyce Spicer
Illustrated by Tim Hayward
Designed by Ian Winton

British Library Cataloguing in Publication Data
Greenaway, Theresa, 1947-
  Spiders. – (Minibeast Pets)
  1. Spiders – Juvenile literature
  2. Invertebrates as pets – Juvenile literature
  I. Title
  595.4'4
HARDBACK   ISBN 0 7502 2509 2
PAPERBACK   ISBN 0 7502 2513 0
Printed and bound in the USA

find Wayland on the Internet at http://www.wayland.co.u

Contents

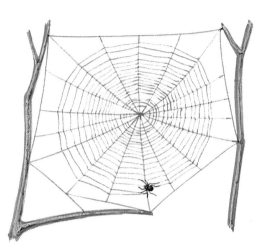

Do you know how to tell a spider from an insect? Just count its legs. An insect has only six legs, but a spider runs around on eight.

Spiders make unusual minibeast pets, and they are easy to keep. Spiders live almost everywhere, so it is not difficult to find them.

A spider's body is divided into two parts, joined by a narrow waist.

The head and all eight legs are at the front. The back part is the spider's abdomen.

How spiders see

Although most spiders have eight small eyes, they have poor eyesight. They can see only changes in darkness and light.

Most spiders spin webs with silk from their spinnerets. The webs are traps to catch prey.

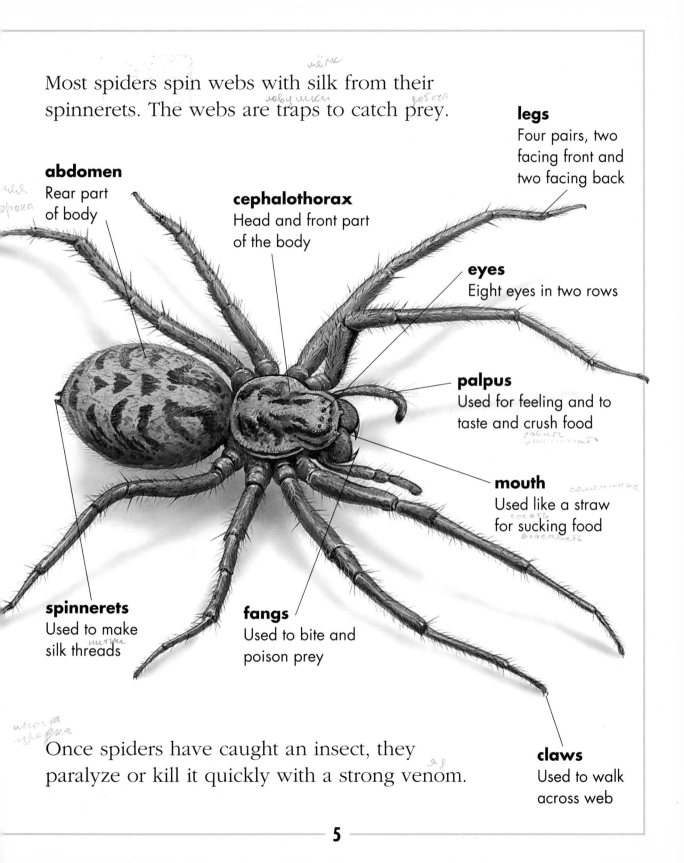

legs
Four pairs, two facing front and two facing back

abdomen
Rear part of body

cephalothorax
Head and front part of the body

eyes
Eight eyes in two rows

palpus
Used for feeling and to taste and crush food

mouth
Used like a straw for sucking food

spinnerets
Used to make silk threads

fangs
Used to bite and poison prey

claws
Used to walk across web

Once spiders have caught an insect, they paralyze or kill it quickly with a strong venom.

Finding spiders

Spiders live wherever they can catch enough food to eat. Once you start looking, you will be amazed at how many there are.

Begin by searching your house. Cupboards are a good place to find spiders that like the dark. Look on windowsills and up in the corners of rooms, too.

Outside, spiders live on lawns, in walls and flowerbeds, and under forgotten flowerpots.

They also live on tree trunks and in garden sheds.

▶ The water spider can live under water in ponds. It carries air down between its back legs and stores it in a dome of stretchy silk.

During your spider hunt, you may find only spiders' webs. But look very carefully. Is there a tunnel of web leading down to a hiding place? Is there a rolled leaf nearby under which the spider could be hiding?

Try gently touching the web with a blade of grass. This will make the spider rush out of its hiding place.

▼ Some spiders spin thick sheets of web in corners. If an insect touches this web, the spider runs out from its hiding place and traps it.

▼ A hammock web is a maze of silk threads. Any insect that falls into it cannot escape quickly. The spider runs easily over the surface and bites its prey.

▼ Large orb webs, which a spider spins in a space between plants or buildings, are the perfect trap for flying insects.

Spider collecting

To collect spiders, you will need several small jars or containers (with air holes in the lids), and a small, soft paintbrush.

Spiders are fragile. Their soft bodies are easily damaged, so try not to touch them with your fingers. Use the paintbrush bristles to guide the spiders gently into different containers. If you put more than one spider in a container, they will eat each other.

Black widow spider

Although it is quite small and shy, the female black widow spider of North America has venom strong enough to kill a person. Anyone bitten by this spider must go straight to hospital for treatment.

Put lids on the containers, and number each one.

Make a list of these numbers in a notebook. Alongside each write the date and where you found the spider. If it had a web, try to describe it.

Identifying spiders

Because there are so many
different kinds of spiders,
trying to identify each of
your new pets may be
tricky. A book on common
spiders will help you.

Using the notes you have made, arrange your spiders
into groups. Here are four of the most common groups:

Orb-web spiders usually live among plants.
They spin round webs that look like wheels.

Running spiders run around on the ground.
Some of them make silk-lined burrows.

Jumping spiders have the largest eyes and the best eyesight of all spiders.

Sheet-web spiders may live indoors or outside. They make a thick sheet of web with a tunnel leading to a hiding place.

▼ This photograph shows three stages of one jumping spider's movements. Jumping spiders jump if they are touched and jump to catch their prey.

Daddy-long-legs spider

One of the easiest spiders to recognize is the daddy-long-legs spider. This harmless spider makes a web in the corner of a room. It has a thin body and amazingly long, thin legs.

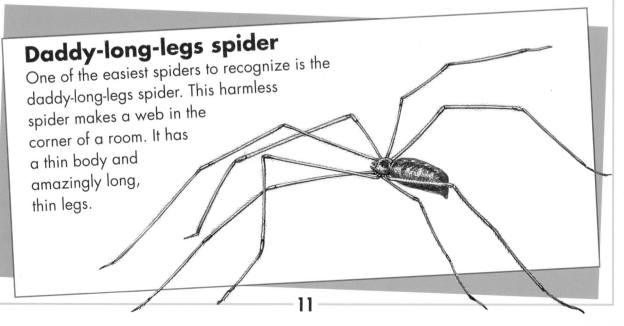

Homes for spiders

You will need a different container to house each spider. An aquarium is best, so that you can see the spider clearly. Each aquarium should have a lid with air holes.

Spread some leaf litter or soil at the bottom of the aquarium.

Add small twigs and plants so that the spider can spin its web and hide.

Purseweb spider

The purseweb spider makes a silk-lined burrow in the ground. This leads into a silk 'purse' that lies along the ground. When an insect walks over the 'purse', the spider bites it through the web and drags it down into the burrow to eat.

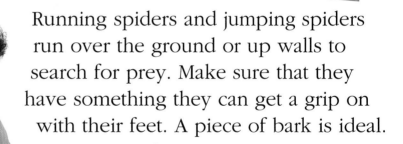

Running spiders and jumping spiders run over the ground or up walls to search for prey. Make sure that they have something they can get a grip on with their feet. A piece of bark is ideal.

Spiders that already live indoors do not really need a new home. But you will have to ask your parents not to dust away the cobwebs for a while!

Caring for spiders

Although spiders can look after themselves, they will need a little help from you.

Make sure their containers are not placed in bright sunlight. Most spiders like some warmth, but they will die if they get too hot.

If you are keeping the containers outside, make sure they are sheltered from rain. Spiders need moisture, but they will drown if their home fills with water. Keep the leaf litter and plants damp, but not waterlogged.

You will need to provide food for your spiders. You can catch flies for them by placing some jam or overripe fruit in a jar. Stand the jar outside. When there are flies inside, put the lid on it.

At feeding time, gently empty the flies into your aquarium.

Hiding and disguising

In the wild, spiders have lots of natural enemies. They often hide, so that birds do not find them. Sometimes they are camouflaged to match their surroundings, which makes them difficult to spot. This crab spider from tropical New Guinea looks just like a fresh bird dropping. No predator wants to eat that!

Watching spiders

One of the most interesting things about spiders is the way each kind makes its web.

Watch your spiders closely using a magnifying glass. See how each one squeezes silk out of the tiny spinnerets at the tip of its abdomen.

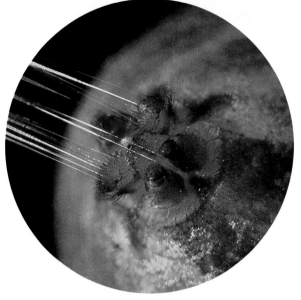

▲ A close-up of a spider's abdomen. The spinnerets are producing silk.

How spiders make their webs

1. A spider shoots out a thread, which catches onto a twig. It then travels along the line, spinning as it goes.

2. Returning to the middle, the spider drops down to attach the line to a twig below.

Once the web is made, the spider hides and waits for a victim.

A single line of silk stretches from the web to the spider's hiding place. When an insect is caught in the web, it begins to struggle. This sends vibrations along the silk thread. The spider feels the vibrations and runs out to snatch its meal.

Spiders never get stuck to their own webs.

Clever catch

The net-throwing spider holds a small web between two pairs of its legs and drops it onto its prey.

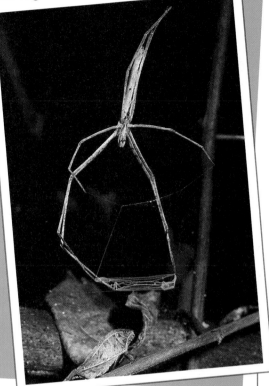

3. Threads are made around the edge of the web and into the centre.

4. The spider makes a spiral to strengthen the web and adds sticky threads for catching prey.

Spiders and their prey

All spiders are carnivores, which means that they attack and eat other living creatures. Find out which insects each of your spiders likes best.

Catch different kinds of flies or other small insects and put them in the webs of your spiders.

Make notes about what happens.

Spiders look busy when they are making a web, but much of their time is spent sitting waiting.

Watch what happens when a fly gets stuck in a spider's web.

▶ This orb-web spider is waiting for an insect to become trapped in its web.

The spider runs out of its hiding place, sinks its fangs into the insect and injects it with venom. This paralyzes it and stops it moving.

Spiders cannot chew. Instead, they dribble saliva onto their food, which dissolves the prey. Then the spider sucks up the soupy insect juices.

▼ A spider makes sure its victim cannot escape by wrapping it in a thick band of silk.

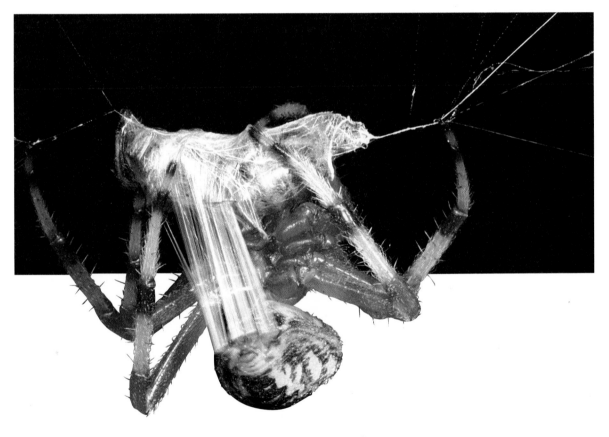

Spiders do not eat insects with an unpleasant taste, such as ladybirds. If a catch isn't good to eat, they either set it free or let it escape.

Spiders do not breed until they are fully grown. In order to get bigger, a spider has to shed its skin. The old skin, or cuticle, splits, and the spider struggles out of it.

Shedding the old skin is called moulting.

▼ This spider has just wiggled free of its old cuticle. It hangs from a silk thread until its new, stretchy skin hardens.

▶ To avoid being mistaken for dinner, a male may take a silk-wrapped fly to the female.

When a female spider is fully grown, she is ready to lay her eggs. She waits for a male spider to find her.

Attracting a mate

Some males make signals with their legs. Others 'pluck' the webs of female spiders.

Finding a mate can be quite risky for a male spider. Males are often much smaller than the females, so a hungry female may mistake him for a meal!

See if you can find a female spider carrying her egg sac, or guarding it in a tent of silk woven around grass stems.

Collect these very carefully, and you may be able to watch the young spiderlings hatch.

When winter comes

Winter is a difficult time for spiders. There are few insects for them to eat, and they have to find a frost-free place to hide away.

Female spiders may lay all their eggs in one batch towards the end of summer. Others may lay several small batches, and then more eggs the following spring.

▲ Wolf spiders cling to their mother until their second moult. If they fall off, they climb back using a thread of silk.

Some spiders guard their eggs until they hatch. Others carry the little spiderlings around for a while.

How long do spiders live?
The average life span of most spiders is about one year, but tarantulas can live up to 30 years.

Spiderlings and adult spiders spend the winter in sheltered places, behind tiles or bark, under logs, or among big tufts of grass.

Go out early on an autumn morning after there has been a frost or heavy dew. Every spider's web will be spangled with droplets of water or ice crystals. You will be surprised to see just how many there are.

▼ A garden spider's web on a frosty winter morning.

Keeping a record

To keep a record of your spiders, you will need a notebook, a magnifying glass and a pencil. Try to find a book on spiders in your library.

Make plenty of notes about your spiders. Include details such as which insects they prefer to eat, and how they catch and wrap up their prey. Note how many times your spiders moult.

Watch how spiders make their webs. When a spider spins a new web it often eats the old one.

▶ As this spider winds up its old web, it eats the silk.

The silk is made of valuable protein, and the spider needs lots of protein to spin its new web.

Spiders have some quite amazing habits. Start a scrapbook, and paste in pictures and articles that you find in magazines.

Once your friends and relatives know you are interested in spiders, they may start collecting for you, too.

Hairy spiders

Seen through a magnifying glass, spiders look hairy. Each hair and bristle is very sensitive to touch. It also picks up tiny vibrations from the air and from the threads of the spider's silk web.

Letting them go

The best time to catch and keep spiders is in the spring and early summer. The weather is warm, and it is easy to catch insects for them to eat.

If the spiders are well fed, they will be fully grown by midsummer. This is a good time to let them go. They can find mates and lay their eggs before the autumn sets in.

Choose a warm, dry day to release your spiders, and return them to the place you found them.

Make sure you let them out somewhere sheltered, or sharp-eyed birds will peck them up.

Stranded spiders

Large house spiders trapped in sinks and baths are a common sight on autumn mornings. They are usually male spiders that have been searching for a female. Once they climb into a sink, the smooth, slippery sides stop them escaping. To help them out, nudge them gently into a container with a soft paintbrush.

Now that you have looked after spiders and made a spider scrapbook, you know how fascinating they are. Why not write a spider quiz for your friends?

Spider facts

Green lynx spiders live in the southern United States and Central America. They live on plants, jumping from one to another. Their colour is a useful camouflage.

There is an Australian spider that uses camouflage to look like a lumpy twig.

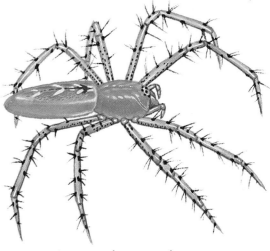

▲ A green lynx spider

The wasp mimic spider looks like a back-to-front wasp. If a bird attacks it, the 'wasp' runs off in an unexpected direction.

◀ A wasp mimic spider

Some people are terrified of spiders – even tiny ones! This uncontrollable fear is called arachnophobia.

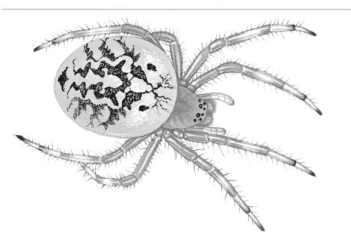

◄ This marbled orb weaver lays orange coloured eggs in the autumn.

Spider silk is amazing. It is made of protein and is stronger than a steel thread of the same thickness. It can stretch to almost double its length before it snaps.

There are over 30,000 different kinds of spiders alive in the world today. The tiniest are no bigger than the head of a pin. The largest spiders are bird-eating, or tarantula, spiders from South America. Their bodies are 8 cm long, and their leg span is 25 cm.

▼ A goldenrod spider can change colour to match the flower in which it is hiding.

Find out if there is a wildlife club or natural history club for children near you. Then, if you find it difficult to identify your spiders, you can take them along to show the experts.

Finding out more

BOOKS

Fun With Science: Minibeasts by
R. Harlow & G. Morgan (Kingfisher, 1998)

I Didn't Know That Spiders Have Fangs
by Claire Llewellyn (Watts, 1997)

My Best Book of Creepy Crawlies by
Claire Llewellyn (Kingfisher, 1998)

*Put Something Beastly in Your Pocket:
Spider* by S. Wiseman (Bookmart, 1996)

*The Really Hairy Scary Spider (and
other creatures with lots of legs)* by
T. Greenaway (Dorling Kindersley, 1998)

VIDEOS

Amazing Animals: Minibeasts
(Dorling Kindersley, 1996)

*Amazing Animals: Creepy Crawly
Animals* (Dorling Kindersley, 1999)

See How They Grow: Minibeasts
(Dorling Kindersley, 1992)

FURTHER INFORMATION

CLEAPPS School Science Service will be
able to help with any aspect of keeping
minibeasts.   Tel: 01895 251496

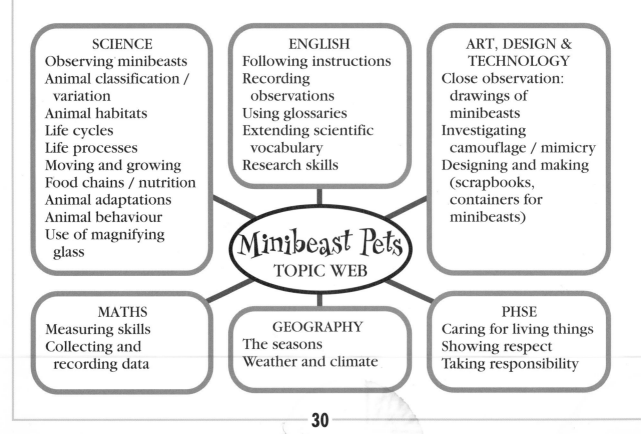

SCIENCE
Observing minibeasts
Animal classification /
   variation
Animal habitats
Life cycles
Life processes
Moving and growing
Food chains / nutrition
Animal adaptations
Animal behaviour
Use of magnifying
   glass

ENGLISH
Following instructions
Recording
   observations
Using glossaries
Extending scientific
   vocabulary
Research skills

**ART, DESIGN &
TECHNOLOGY**
Close observation:
   drawings of
   minibeasts
Investigating
   camouflage / mimicry
Designing and making
   (scrapbooks,
   containers for
   minibeasts)

**Minibeast Pets
TOPIC WEB**

MATHS
Measuring skills
Collecting and
   recording data

GEOGRAPHY
The seasons
Weather and climate

PHSE
Caring for living things
Showing respect
Taking responsibility

Glossary

abdomen The rear part of a spider or insect's body that contains its stomach, guts and reproductive organs.

breed To have young.

camouflage The colouring and patterns on an animal's body that help it to blend in with its surroundings, so that it cannot be seen easily by predators.

identify To find out the name of something.

leaf litter A layer of fallen leaves, mostly from trees.

mimic Something that copies the appearance or behaviour of another kind of animal or plant.

paralyze To make helpless, unable to move or feel anything.

predator An animal that hunts and kills another animal for food.

prey An animal that is hunted and eaten by another animal.

protein One of a group of chemicals that are made by all living things.

saliva The liquid produced in the mouth of an animal.

spinnerets Organs in a spider that produce threads of silk.

venom A poisonous substance that an animal injects into its prey.

vibrations Tiny movements.

Index

The publishers would like to thank the following for their permission to reproduce photographs:
cover George McCarthy/Bruce Coleman, 4 B. Borrell/Frank Lane Picture Agency, 6 G. I. Bernard/Oxford
Scientific Films, 9 Breck P. Kent/Oxford Scientific Films, 11 Kim Taylor/Bruce Coleman, 15 Ken Preston-Mafham/
Premaphotos Wildlife, 16 Dr Frieder Sauer/Bruce Coleman, 17 Ken Preston-Mafham/Premaphotos Wildlife,
18 Ken Preston Mafham/Premaphotos Wildlife, 19 B.G. Murray/Oxford Scientific Films, 20 Rudie Kuiter/Oxford
Scientific Films, 21 top Ken Preston-Mafham/Premaphotos Wildlife, 21 bottom Jane Burton/Bruce Coleman,
22 Ken Preston-Mafham/Premaphotos Wildlife, 23 Ken Preston-Mafham/Premaphotos Wildlife,
24 Kim Taylor/Bruce Coleman, 25 Ingo Arndt/Bruce Coleman, 27 Andrew J. Purcell/Bruce Coleman